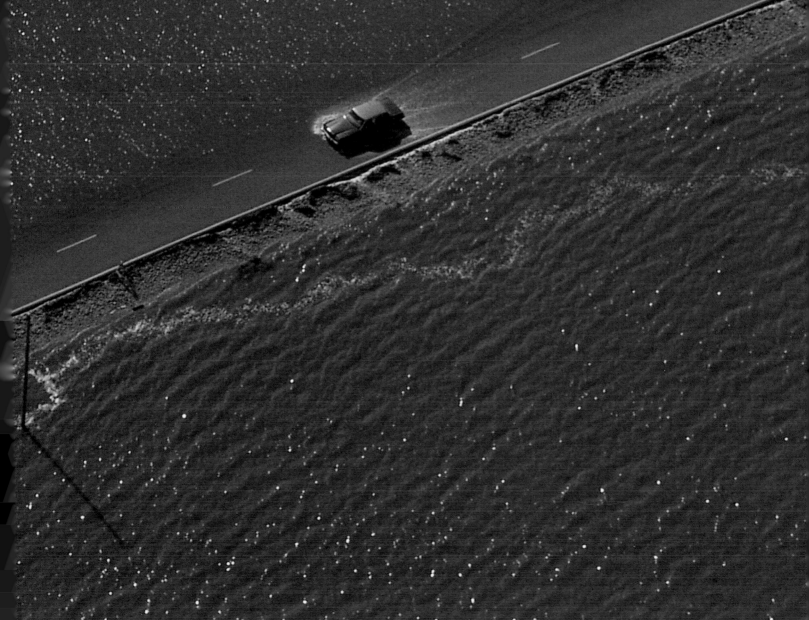

Raging
RIVER

By The Staff Of The Quad City Times
Written by Bill Wundram

The staff of the *Quad-City Times*
Story by Bill Wundram
Quad-City Times photos by Craig Chandler, Jeff Cook,
   Greg Boll, John Schultz, Leslie Hahn, Shane Keyser
   and Larry Fisher.
Aerial photos by Larry Mayer of The Billings, Mont.,
   Gazette
Graphics by Craig Chandler
Edited by Daniel K. Hayes

© 1993 The Quad-City Times,
500 E. 3rd St., Davenport, IA 52801.

Published by the Quad-City Times
Robert A. Fusie, Publisher
Daniel K. Hayes, Editor

Library of Congress Catalog Card Number 93-072708

ISBN 0-9627618-4-2

Design: Ben Leonard
Cover photo by Larry Mayer
Coordinated by The Billings Gazette
Design, typesetting and printing by
   Fenske Printing Inc., Billings, Montana

For additional copies of this book, contact:

The Quad-City Times
"Raging River Book"
500 E. 3rd Street
Davenport, IA 52801

To order by phone, call Toll Free
   1-800-543-2707

*On the cover:
Davenport's levee
playground and central
business district, awash
in the Great Flood of
1993.*

*Page 1: A farm north
of Muscatine becomes
an island in the
swollen Iowa River.*

*Pages 2 & 3: A car
churns a boat-like
wake as its driver
struggles through
overflow of the Rock
River near Moline.*

*Pages 6 & 7: Only the
tops of trees mark
what once were islands
near Andalusia, Ill.*

Foreword

Adversity is the true test of character. Iowans met the challenge of the Flood of '93 with courage, hard work and a determination not to let the worst natural disaster in our state's history prevent us from helping each other to move ahead.

I am proud of the way Iowans showed their willingness to help each other win this battle.

Neighbors helped neighbors. People who suffered losses helped others who were still in the fight. The outpouring of volunteers and contributions bolstered our efforts to save lives, protect property, clean up the mess and restore life to normal.

Iowans are grateful for the support from throughout the nation. We are united in our indomitable spirit to succeed despite adversity.

Terry E. Branstad

Terry E. Branstad, Governor of Iowa

One of the worst natural disasters in our state's history brought out the best in our people.

The entire nation was witness to a valiant effort to save homes, businesses and some of the best farmland in the world from rivers on the rampage.

Bankers and farmers, National Guard members and prisoners, state workers and local officials, senior citizens and kids engaged the swollen rivers, lakes and streams of Illinois state side by side, shoulder to shoulder.

I was especially moved when farmers who had fought for weeks to protect their crops and homes — only to see their efforts turn to naught — moved to still another battlefront to help others avoid similar devastation.

Now, perhaps a greater challenge lies before us. We must recover and rebuild community by community, family by family. And I am convinced we will prevail because of the spirit and the character of our people.

Jim Edgar

Jim Edgar, Governor of Illinois

CONTENTS

Left: Scott Sappington of East Moline helps build a sandbag wall in Moline.

Introduction

Looking down upon a sea

His "old man of the river" face wrinkled with worry. The skies drizzled with summer rain and he was hurrying to move out — the water was rising a foot a day around his home down on Davenport's South Concord. Jim VanFossen, who has lived on the Mississippi River for 70 of his 79 years, had a phrase: "It's as bad as it can be." The river around him was a stage that was set for tragedy.

Jim VanFossen "got out" and finally his river sprawled everywhere in a torrent that was the "Mother of All Floods" — a record 22.63 feet in Davenport. About 7 1/2 feet above flood stage. The vast watershed region for hundreds of miles, up, down and around the Quad-Cities was an ocean. It was breathtaking and miserable, an overpowering rush, pushing 260,000 cubic feet of the water per second downstream.

I flew over the state of Iowa and circled across the debris-sloshed range of the Mississippi River into Illinois. The Mississippi, and every river that flows into it, looked to bulge five to 10 miles out of their banks. It was almost a perversity of humor. Smaller tributary streams were running backward because the drowning Mississippi was rushing into them. Every creek was washed far and wide over farmlands, spreading like tentacles into fields that never will see the plow this year. I have never seen so much water in America. I sensed that I was looking down upon a sea. In the past, we patiently lived with floods. The channel could be arbitrary, with its own tempo. It often flooded in the springtime and eased back to its willow-shaded banks in the summer. The year 1993 was tragically different. There was unrelenting rain. There was an irksome crest in early spring. It was a spring rise that never quite went away. In early July it crested once. Then, it drowned us with a double punch — still another higher crest.

River Drive became just that in downtown Davenport.

11

SPECIAL EDITION: FLOOD OF 1993 REACHES ITS CREST

METRO EDITION
Quad-City
Times

88° 70° Warm Details 4A

SATURDAY, July 3, 1993
QUAD-CITY TIMES

FLOOD WATCH: The Mississippi is at 21.8 feet.

50 CENTS

THIS IS IT!

And we can hope the worst is over

By Lee Nelson and Scott Reeder
QUAD-CITY TIMES

The crest.
We've awaited it with wariness, wondering just what final troubles it will cause. But in a way, we also welcome it today, knowing it signals the beginning of the end.
The Mississippi River will etch its way into the history books once again if it reaches the predicted 22-foot level — second only to the Great Flood of 1965.
Gary Grabin looks through his window in Hampton, Ill., with candles burning. He has high hopes the river will stop rising today so his life and the lives of everyone affected by the 1993 flood can possibly, slowly, begin to get back to normal.
"We're surrounded by water, and our basement is filled. We're just camping out in our own house. We haven't had electricity since Wednesday," Grabin said.

"Sometimes, you get a little seasick hearing the water constantly slosh against the walls."
Disaster workers hope the couple of extra inches of water that will rise overnight will not cause more hardships.

■ DAMAGE ESTIMATES
Assessments of the damage cannot be
— FLOOD
Please turn to Page 2A

INSIDE
■ Bill Wundram's sandbag sagas 2A
■ A look up and down the river 3A
■ Gibbs, Garden Addition residents clash ... 4A
■ President Clinton might bring help 5A
■ Road closings, where to call for help 5A
■ The view from the air 6A
■ The crest might linger for a day 7A
■ Inmates shore up Keithsburg dike 7A

Ann Landers .... 7W   Obituaries 2M
Business .... 9A-11A   Record 3M
Classifieds ..... 3M-14M   Recreation 8B
Illinois .... 12A   Religion 14A
Iowa .... 12A   Sports 1B-8B
Lottery .... 2A   World 13A
Nation .... 8A   Wundram 2A

The levees or flood walls punctured repeatedly with what is called a "crevasse." That is a break, a single word that meant dread and panic, for it allowed water to burst across cities and fields.
It was, without anyone's question, far more dreadful than the oft-remembered "Great Flood of 1965" that crested at 22.48, compared to 1993's 22.63. This "Great Flood of 1993" stayed, angered and stretched our patience like an overwrought fiddle string. There was sorrow and humor, despair and hope, calm and panic and anger. Mostly, it was disbelief. Their old friend, the Mississippi River, with its Mark Twain-esque attraction, showed once again that the foregone is always there. It renewed the fear that the Mississippi is not always the coziest of friends. It proved, as we always knew, that all of us are quite puny in the face of such catastrophes.

Top left: Big headlines shout the first crest, but the worst is yet to come.

Above: In Keithsburg, Ill., Rick Percy struggles to move belongings from his garage.

The record flood

Rain, rain, rain:
No moment in the sun

It rained cats and dogs in the middle of June in the flat farmland country of Marshall, Minn., pouring a cloudburst of 12 inches onto the land in 30 hours. Less than a week later, another 11 inches drenched a place called Fairmount, in southern Minnesota.

It rained, and it rained, and it rained. All that water was dumped — like nature's most unforgiving bucket — into the watershed of the Father of Waters, making it mightier and more muscle-bound than ever before.

The Quad-Cities had been drenched by unrelenting rainfall since early springtime, leaving the ground bloated and unwilling to accept any new water, which now was cascading toward us from Minnesota. It was a prelude to a catastrophe along the Mississippi River. Most disasters come and end quickly. The record 1993 flood crept toward us slowly and was reluctant to leave. There was a curious silence. It did not always race across the land, as one may depict a flood, but often moved at its own leisure. Everyone who lived through the "Great Flood of 1993" will have its eeriness, its unsettling manner, its chilling effect, forever etched in memory. Like all catastrophes, it was ruthless, finally giving up at 22.63 feet in the Quad-Cities. After that, the American Red Cross rated this flood a Level Five Disaster, its most severe status. Hurricane Andrew in Florida was a Level Five. On the day it crested in Davenport last July 9, at more than 7 1/2 feet above flood level, Gary Grabin stared out his window at Hampton, Ill. Candles flickered to light his house. He spoke passively: "We're surrounded by water. We're just camping out in our own house. We haven't had electricity since the middle of the week. Sometimes, you get a little seasick hearing the water constantly slosh against the walls." The wallop turned far worse than the "Great Flood of 1965," which was touted to be the "Flood of the Century." In 1965, the Quad-Cities

Left: Harry Pells of Bettendorf carries fuel for the pumps keeping his office dry at Perry Street and River Drive in Davenport. They needed to be refueled every 90 minutes.

crested at 22.48 feet. In 1993, it scaled to a crest of 22.63.The "Flood of '93" created a vast, unreal waterway, leaving behind seas of mucky smelly swamps in fields and fetid pockets of stinking sewage water on sloppy, slick streets. Fish flopped a few feet from Davenport Firstar Bank, where pumps hummed in the basement. Some fishermen dropped long lines and bobbers into the deep water beside Davenport Perry Street Parking Building. Minnows swam in little whirlpools. Landmarks like the Davenport riverfront LeClaire Park — a merry arena for national fests like "The Blues" and "The Bix" — were left useless for the season. Muscatine, cramped for parking places and with enough other flood misery on its mind, pulled the plug to cancel its Great River Days. The flood agonized.

"With 30 inches of water, and an inch of dirt and mud on everything, it was enough to make a grown man cry," said Ahmad Vossoughi, who had the Oasis Convenience Store on Second Street in Davenport. The flood left some houses so swamped that only chimneys and rooftops stuck above the water, and living room drapes floated like fish nets in flooded homes of Keithsburg, Ill. It filled basements with six feet of water. Lifetimes of personal

treasures were lost in oozing muck. Some Campbell's Island residents in East Moline, unable to rescue washers and dryers from basements, listened to them bumping and floating against cellar ceilings. Between the muddy carpeting and damp mattresses and soaked sofas, John and Sue Wendt managed a sigh.

"I woke up at 6:30 one morning, thinking that this was a bad dream," Sue said. "The water was rushing in all over. I bawled and bawled." A broken dike along U.S. 6 had gushed into Quad-City Partnership Mobile Home Park, Coal Valley, Ill. While

Above: As levels climb, Rick Corbin, Steve Eis and Larry Winkeman pile sandbags to keep floodwaters out of Chet's Tavern and the Heritage House Floor & Wall Shop at the foot of the Government Bridge in Davenport.

Above right: Like a marooned white whale, The President Riverboat — its slot machines silent — waits out of harm's way.

they tried to dry-out bedding, a neighbor, Linda Vancourt, sloshed in water up to her knees in the street.

The record "Great Flood of 1993" began prophetically slow, a rise that first lapped over the walls of Davenport LeClaire Park and sent the big President riverboat casino scurrying upstream to safer portage, and finally — far upriver in Bettendorf — to anchor-out the flood while its slot machines quit jangling and its poker chips stacked in silence. It would be weeks before the casino could kick up its heels again. On June 27, a few Davenport streets and Moline's River Drive closed. So, it was another flood. Nothing new about floods in the Quad-Cities, but the rising waters of the summer of 1993 seemed particularly menacing.

The Dock Restaurant, only 10 days under new ownership, gurgled in deep water. The manager and utility people glided inside by boat and rowed beside the bar to turn off the power. D.L. "Skip" Anderson, the new owner, weakly joked: "We could have plenty of fresh fish on our menu."

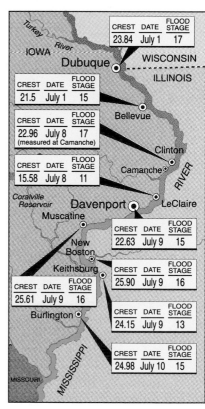

CREST	DATE	FLOOD STAGE
23.84	July 1	17

Dubuque

CREST	DATE	FLOOD STAGE
21.5	July 1	15

Bellevue

CREST	DATE	FLOOD STAGE
22.96	July 8	17
(measured at Camanche)

Clinton

CREST	DATE	FLOOD STAGE
15.58	July 8	11

Camanche

LeClaire

Davenport

Muscatine

CREST	DATE	FLOOD STAGE
22.63	July 9	15

New Boston

Keithsburg

CREST	DATE	FLOOD STAGE
25.90	July 9	16

CREST	DATE	FLOOD STAGE
25.61	July 9	16

CREST	DATE	FLOOD STAGE
24.15	July 9	13

Burlington

CREST	DATE	FLOOD STAGE
24.98	July 10	15

MISSOURI

MISSISSIPPI

Previous page: In a rare moment without rain, sunlight sparkles on the Davenport riverfront. At lower right is the Dock restaurant, where water flows over the top of the bar.

Above: A tractor sits atop the pitcher's mound in Davenport's John O'Donnell Stadium. At the height of the flood, it will be partially submerged.

Above right: John O'Donnell Stadium, home of the Quad-City River Bandits — a total strikeout for the baseball season.

Classy John O'Donnell Stadium, remodeled just a few years ago, became an icon of the flood as water filled field and dugouts. It slumped into a soaking strikeout. The Quad-City River Bandits moved their home games to North Scott High, a "field of dreams" where you brought your own lawn chair and a swatted homer could end in a cornfield. No question, we ominously faced a big flood. But in July? Floods are supposed to come in the springtime. By June 30, residents in $150,000 homes along Harbor Drive in Pleasant Valley stood waist-deep in their back yards, disbelieving what was happening to green lawns they normally would be mowing. A cheerless announcement on that last day of June came from the National Weather Service: June had been the rainiest month in Quad-City history. Storms kept booming thunder and lightning upstream, brim-filling the already overloaded tributaries like the Wapsipinicon.

"Sandbags, where are the sandbags?" went the cry. "More sand, more sand." A half-million sandbags were rushed to Scott and Rock Island counties, to be loosely packed and tightly tied.

"One of the spookiest night scenes that I remember early in the flood," said Davenport Mayor Pat Gibbs, "was a bumper-to-bumper honking caravan of six giant city trucks, mounded so high with sand that it spilled onto streets. Police cars with flashing lights and sirens guarded the front and back of the peculiar parade. They were rushing to fill a boil in the dike in the Village of East Davenport." Davenport city streets had a sound of their own, the scrunch of grinding sand, spilled from dump trucks, hurrying to build dikes. Into town rushed the Na-

tional Guard, lumbering, smiling guys, anxious workers whose backs never seemed to ache. Police and city workers went on 12- or 14-hour daily duty. A 10-day warning had sounded a flood alarm, and 140 remote stations fed frightening reports every 15 minutes from the 80,000 square mile watershed of the Rock Island District, U.S. Army Corps of Engineers.

The fickle river frightened and told no plans. First, a crest of 18 feet — three feet above flood level — then 19 feet, and Moline, for the first time in history, called off its Riverfest. Ben Butterworth Memorial Parkway in Moline swirled in a mass of jumbled trees, old tires and barrels, while Davenport's River Drive became a vast, open lake, stretching for five miles and lapping as far as Third Street.

The rumored cry went up, "It's going to be worse than 1965," and Bill Koellner, chief of the Water Con-

Above: Convoys of trucks haul sand to make floodwalls in the Village of East Davenport.

trol Section for the Corps of Engineers, cautiously said that it might.

There was simply too much water for too little space, and so the Mississippi spread and swamped and inched into the lowlands while the skies emptied with nearly daily rainfall. A murky, inevitable, rain-a-day gloom settled over an edgy Quad-Cities.

Leota Buffington of Buffalo, Iowa, never saw it shower so regularly. She said: "In bright summer sunshine, I would go into the supermarket to buy a few items. When I came out, rain would be pouring down for the rest of the day."

A drizzly 4th of July soaked us into a damp fizzle. Prophetstown, Ill., was in a funk. The town, reknown for its dazzling rockets red glare, reluctantly canceled an annual fireworks display. The kids sulked. Davenport's Credit Island Park, always a popular holiday picnic spa, looked to be floating away. From the air, it was invisible as the city's biggest park.

Flood-swept cities up and down the Mississippi dropped deeper into the water on that dismal July 4,

1993, when the Mississippi climbed to its first crest — 22.03 feet — in the Quad-Cities.

But there was no ending, no moment in the sun in the surge. More water, higher water, would come. Some force appeared to be tinkering with us. The flood's topping off changed daily, almost hourly, and industries and homes braced for losing battles. Even the mail faced a problem of getting through.

"We're going to high ground," said Davenport Postmaster Dan Foley, moving the post office to the gaunt, vacant old Sears, Roebuck building on West Fourth Street. Surrounded by water, McGinnis Chambers & Sass Funeral Home in Bettendorf locked its doors for the first time. There was a sick joke around town that they were offering burials at sea. They had switched their services to Asbury United Methodist, where the faithful — as in all Quad-City churches — prayed every Sabbath for deliverance from this flood. Already, Davenport's Garden Addition — a tract of trim small homes that was stunned by water up to its rooftops in the Flood of 1965 — had been evacuated. A dike had

Above left: Six-year-old Dwayne Smith of Joslin, Ill., helps relatives fill sandbags in Keithsburg, Ill.

Above: Mud, water, sand and sweat — the reward for flood volunteers.

Next page: A half-million sandbags were filled in the Quad-Cities. Volunteers were given free tickets to Bon Jovi at The Mark of the Quad-Cities.

been built after 1965, but the Davenport city guardians were edgy. Would it hold? No one held bets. Twenty police officers organized the exodus of 600 to 700 people late one dreary afternoon. The Garden Addition people took haven with relatives, friends or at the Red Cross shelter in the Army Reserve Armory on Division Street. The evacuation was a testy time for the city. Those who insisted on staying did so as long as they remained on their own property. Their confrontations with the mayor, police and National Guardsmen did not ease the agitation in the sticky, sweaty days of July 1993. Mosquitoes buzzed from the green backwaters of Nahant Slough, a few miles down the road. In Garden Addition, Don Fuller shouted angrily: "It's my property. I don't have to leave if I don't want to. It's my constitutional right to stay here and I'm going to." He stayed. The city worried that the mushy dike would collapse and engulf the 20 residents who chose to hold out in their homes. Water crept to the edge of some streets, but the dike held.

Traffic in Davenport lurched slowly, barely under control. Detours became a migrained agony. Tempers flared in the honking, bumper-to-bumper snarls that twisted up and down hills through unfamiliar streets.

Flood watchers came from afar. There was no way to keep them away. Was this not the flood of the century? They wanted to take a look. This flood became the flood of the camcorder. Staring crowds were mesmerized by the swift flow of the Mississippi River. They stood in unseemly lines along railings of the Centennial Bridge. Normally, at this season, the river would be lazing along at a mile or

Above : Mildred Shoemaker retrieves what she can from her home in Keithsburg, Ill.

No otter in the water

By yawn's early light, a CNN commentator interviewed Davenport Mayor Pat Gibbs beside the beleaguered Davenport Ground Transportation Center. Cameras zoomed in on a water-soaked animal, scurrying from the water.

"There," said the announcer, "is an otter, escaping the floodwaters."

The mayor interrupted.

"Sorry, but that's no otter. It's a big river rat."

Above: Tempers flared in Davenport's Garden Addition when residents learned they could not return to the homes they were ordered to evacuate. Arguing with Davenport Mayor Pat Gibbs, right, is Bob Conner.

Right: A woman uses a video camera to capture the flood-swollen Iowa River as it claims a house below Highway 99 in Wapello. Muscatine Journal photo by Tom Korte

Whoops!

With all the media attention to Davenport, some boners had to rise above the water. An announcer for CNN said the water had hit 22 feet above flood stage in Davenport. That would put the flood at about Kimberly Road and Brady Street, spilling into Northpark Shopping Center.

Left: A mural of jazz great - and Davenport native - Bix Beiderbecke gets a bath as floodwaters lap against the parking ramp at Second and Perry Streets in Davenport. The ramp was a popular spot for flood watchers.

two an hour. Now, it was speeding at a silent dozen miles an hour. Rooftops and even autos swirled downstream. The flood-watchers dashed back and forth against the bridge traffic, some pushing baby strollers. Police finally banned sightseers from the bridge, with its entrances sandbagged against a water-filled Second Street that slowed Centennial Bridge traffic to a single lane. With the Government Bridge closed, and its toll booths fed by tourists, Centennial Bridge traffic doubled during the Great Flood of 1993.

Everywhere, there lingered despair. Even folks living along the Mississippi, who had been suckled by floods, showed fear. But everyone, it seemed, took pity. At the National Women's Choral Festival in Cincinnati, Ohio, 650 voices sang a paean of hope to the Quad-Cities. On July 5, the cocoa-colored river inched a slight descent. In celebration, Juanita Sawyer floated rubber alligators and water toys around the sandbagged J&J locks near the Davenport side of the Government Bridge.

The crucial doom was flowing south, but the worst was yet to arrive in the Quad-Cities. Rains of the north would not relent, and bold headlines forecast another crest — still higher — for a numbed

Davenport and the cities downstream. It would rise to 22.4, the Corps of Engineers said, outdistancing the 22.03 crest of July 4.

Elizabeth Dole, president of the American Red Cross, flew into the Quad-Cities to bolster volunteers. Iowa Gov. Terry Branstad said: "I know of no area that is totally spared." The weary, flood-worn Quad-Cities watched and anxiously waited. Not only the Mississippi, but Rock River had long ago worn out its welcome. On July 8, Grace Dorbeck said: "This is the sixth Rock River crest this year." She has been a neighbor to the Rock for 46 years. "I'd just like to pack up and leave but my husband, Chris, won't go." The Rock ran 2 1/2 feet above flood stage. Grace had moved all their furniture to the upstairs of their home, but she worried about the unknown. Rivers have no conscience. Davenport became a dubious celebrity. Media from all over the world converged upon "the flood city." Programs like "Good Morning America" and "Today" and "Nightline" televised twice from Davenport — once, as it poured through the city, and again during the massive, muddy cleanup. Charles Kuralt's "Sunday Morning" spent a lot of time in Davenport. Quad-City Times editor Dan Hayes appeared with other

JUNE 25

JUNE 27

JUNE 28

JUNE 30

JULY 3

JULY 7

JULY 9, 1993

Left and above: The Iowa Pork Stop, a popular riverfront hotdog stand, became a visual indicator of the rising waters. The series of photos was taken from June 25, top left, through July 9, when the flood crested in Davenport at 22.6 feet. At right shows the high-water mark in the flood of 1965.

APRIL 28, 1965

flood-weary editors on the MacNeil/Lehrer news hour. On a flight leaving Russia, views of beleaguered, flooded Davenport, Iowa, filled a TV screen. Europeans shook their heads. Davenport residents found themselves answering anxious telephone calls from friends and relatives all over the world. On July 9, 1993, the long, agonizing wait ended. Lastly, bitterly, the Mississippi River crested in the Quad-Cities at 22.63 feet, an all-time, whopping-wet high. The moment between the present, and the future's shadow, had come face-to-face. The crest surged, but was generally serene, and not quite quiet. A flood crest is not a noisy, booming catastrophe. Quad-Citians had gone through so much, for so long, that the crest was almost anti-climactic. On that day, Dee Kettler who lives on 49th Street in Moline, abandoned her home. "I live two blocks from the river. I never thought it would get in my home." On Campbell's Island, where half the 150 homes were in water, residents had been given the choice of staying or quitting the swamped place. Those who chose to stay walked the bridge (unsafe for cars) and waded through swift, waist-deep water.

"It's awful," said Gene Herrington, a Campbell's Island resident, carrying two bags of groceries while wading through the churning brown foam. The flood had touched every city along the Mississippi and even its tiniest tributaries — towns and cities like Dubuque, Bellevue, Green Island, Savanna, Sabula, Clinton, Fulton, Cordova, Princeton, LeClaire, Rapids City, Hampton, Andalusia, Buffalo, Montpelier, Muscatine, Wapello, New Boston, Keithsburg, Oakville, Oquawka, Burlington, Fort Madison, Keokuk — all the way of the route of the flooded waterway of a highway.

Above: Freemie Shoemaker, center, and cousin Kenny Jackson push their belongings for Mildred and John Shoemaker as they evacuate their home in Keithsburg, Ill.

Right: Only the bravest stayed behind on Campbell's Island, East Moline. The only way in or out was by boat.

Above: Davenport firefighters Gary Kaasa and Joe Smith blast away the mud and silt on Third Street as the slow work of street cleanup began.

Sunrise where the river runs from east to west, at the edge of Davenport.

It was indeed, a tragedy of our times, but along the Mississippi, some would say that it could have been worse. In Des Moines, 250,000 people went without safe drinking water or running water for showers or toilets for more than a week. Electricity had been shut off at times to as many as 30,000 customers.

After drifting past the Quad-Cities, the crest traveled a dozen miles a day to the harassed cities downstream. At West Quincy, Mo., a crossroads in the torrent, the bulwark of a levee blew at 8 p.m. one night, swallowing 10,000 more acres and sending people racing from their homes and businesses. Flames lit the sky in a hellish, flooding inferno when a gas station on the river exploded. It became a catastrophe of helpless proportions, stranding thousands. Bayview Bridge at West Quincy closed — the only river crossover for 200 miles from Burlington, Iowa, to St. Louis, Mo. Around the Quad-Cities, the agonizing cleanup began. The "flood that wouldn't leave" lingered on streets,

collapsing dry walled homes, warping floors in a smelly, disheartening mess. A Davenport city worker, weary after sandbagging, took to flushing off the muddy streets. He said: "We're scrubbing streets with ammonia, but they still smell like outhouses." Water that made an island of downtown Davenport's Riverview Inn swirled down the storm sewers and the hotel put on its marquee, "Guests Welcome." Water receded from O'Donnell Stadium, leaving the emerald outfield a mucky mass of coffee-colored grass. Damage estimates soared into the billions. Those who were hit filled out forms for federal assistance. Likely, the losses will never be fully assessed. It is difficult to tabulate misery. Chasing away the blues, the Quad-City Times Bix 7, one of the nation's major running races, forgot adversity and attracted 16,859 runners to Davenport. There was water around the downtown edges, but the fair-like crowds were merry in homage to Bix Beiderbecke, Davenport's late, lamented young man with a horn. Jazz bands hit their high notes by

Left: Mitch Hagge, 5, shows off one of the dozen carp that he and his dad, Kenny, caught in an hour while fishing from the loading dock Petersen-Hagge Furniture in Davenport.

switching concerts to high and dry locations, far from the draining riverfront.

Through all the double, double, toil and trouble, there arose anew the question of beauty or the beast? While Davenport was doused and drowned, and parts of Moline got a soaking, Rock Island smugly sat high and dry, even holding a street festival while its cousins across the river in Davenport bailed water. Rock Island had built a floodwall after being socked in 1965; Clinton, Iowa, did too, leaving the city secure from the raging river. Muscatine, with perhaps a paranoid fear of flooding from places like Mad Creek, erected permanent dikes and flood gates.

Davenport hadn't built a wall. Neither did Moline. Davenport, the hardest hit in 1993, always wanted to maintain its reputation as having the most beautiful waterfront on the Mississippi River.

"Historically, it has been aesthetics vs. protection," said former Davenport Mayor Thom Hart. Davenport has been twice-chastened. Will a good scare be worth more to a city than good advice? Fear, they say, is the father of courage and the mother of safety. River people are a breed of their own. As the flood ebbed in Davenport, Bob Fitzgibbon stood sweating in waders and up to his knees in water. He answered the telephone at his AAA Muffler Shop on rain-swollen Second Street. "Can I make an appointment for a new muffler?" the caller asked. "Just as soon as we get the water out. Maybe in a week," he answered. "I'll call you back." He noticed that swimming in his office was a big carp.

Right: The American flag flies in front of AAA Muffler in Davenport while an employee watches the flood waters rise to the tops of sandbags.

Small towns under siege by the rivers

Left: Devastated Keithsburg, Ill., the morning after the levee broke. The Mississippi crested 10 feet above flood stage, submerging two-thirds of the town.

Following pages: Marooned cattle huddle along the Iowa River near Muscatine.

"I had hope, but when I heard the sirens, I knew the levee was gone." Carole Willits, of Keithsburg, Ill., wept, broken-hearted. "It's pure shock — it's a horror to watch your house going." For some small towns, the fight against flooding had an inevitable ending. While their big-city cousins upstream were at least holding some ground, smaller cities downstream faced wholesale terror. The choppy Mississippi River, whipped by winds and fed by showers, pushed waves over the top of bulwark dikes mushy from weeks of rain or even pitted with gopher holes. Sandbags bolstered the weak boils, but the Mississippi's rampaging torrent, and the surge of other rivers, relentlessly pounded the small towns. Rural levees broke into crevasses of water that spilled into the towns.

The bigger cities got the headlines and the TV flashes, but the little towns suffered miserably. Keithsburg, 900 people and about 40 miles downstream from the Quad-Cities, despaired in a surge of water that uprooted trees and sent barns topsyturvy, flooding two-thirds of the town's homes and businesses and leaving some despaired residents with an attitude that it was "a water-logged ghost town." The river topped out at 10 feet above flood stage.

The week before the crest, worshipers knelt in Keithsburg churches in prayer that the dikes would hold. This time, even prayer couldn't help. Water, punching through weakened floodwalls, inundated First Christian Church. The following Sunday, emotional services shifted to St. Mary's Catholic Church which had escaped high water. National Guardsmen slept in the basement.

Other towns lost, too, but none with quite the intensity of Keithsburg. At least 200 Keithsburg homes "drowned," some to the rafters and rooftops.

Most had no electricity when weakened levees erupted in a rapidly rising swell of water on July 7 and 8. All the stores closed, even the Casey's General Store, a mainstay of the town. No food. No water. Not even a place to buy a Pepsi. Boats shuttled residents. "It was like watching your whole town sink under water," said Mike Abbot, as the levees faltered. The tragedy to a town like Keithsburg will not go away. "This town won't survive without federal assistance," Boyd Shaw said. He was grim. He looked at his boots, caked with mud. "Keithsburg, as we know it, and I have lived here 18 years, won't exist after this flood. People have had it . . ." "You could never know such misery," said Sharon Reason, Keithsburg city clerk. Keithsburg ached. The city hurt and hungered. From Aledo, Ill., came food, disposable diapers and bottles of water. In one weekend, sweating Keithsburg flood workers went through 18 cases of Gatorade. Desperate for water, Keithsburg dug a new well when the water ebbed. The receding water revealed a mud-slick town. At Oquawka, Ill., where 200,000 sandbags barricaded the streets , they gave free tetanus shots on Main Street. The levees looked like bunkers in an anguished war zone. Everywhere, on this wild river — from Dubuque to Davenport to Muscatine and beyond — the river spewed a fetid cesspool of potential illness. As far north as St. Paul, Minn., cities dumped their raw sewage into this floodplain. It smelled, an ugly unforgiven smell.

One night in Oquawka, the city council cut its meeting short so the council could rush out and enforce the west side of the levee. The new North Pier Marina, built for $50,000, bobbed like a cork under a dozen feet of water. Don Ostrander took a boat to look inside his marina's bar. He could barely see, but managed to spot the carpeting and a few bottles afloat.

Above: Working side by side, residents and National Guard troops sandbag in Oquawka, Ill.

The quiet shores of Oquakwa, Ill., become a rush of activity as the crest nears.

Left: Iowa's "Island City," Sabula becomes exactly that.

Above: Christopher Pizano, 6, walks with relatives Octavio and Francis across the entryway to Campbell's Island after flooding closed the only road onto the island.

Right: On July 6, 1993, Oquawka, Ill., was almost out of measuring stick as the Mississippi River neared crest level.

Worried, frightened and rain-soaked, 300 people hurriedly evacuated Gulfport, Ill., when two of its three levees gave out. The 4th of July parade switched to a sandbagging brigade and the charcoaled pork chops to be sold at the picnic became supper for volunteers.

Sabula, holding claim to tourists as being Iowa's only "Island City," surged into a truly river-locked city. Bridges closed and more than 150 homes, 18 apartments and four businesses got a severe soaking.

In Buffalo, Iowa, where water crept to 200 homes, they tried to laugh through their tears. They named their pumps Little Bob, Big Bob, Little Joe and Big Bertha. At the Whistlestop Inn, Judy O'Neal said:

"People wondered when we said Little Joe wasn't looking so good. It just meant that he was clogged." Downstream, day after day under drenching skies, National Guardsmen had kept the Iowa River at bay, but gave up when the force of still another break in the levee slammed a two-story farm house off its foundation and floated it into a clump of trees. Around Louisa County, in Iowa, 2,000 people evacuated their homes. All of Oakville, a small neighborly town, reluctantly left under National Guard orders. Volunteers raced door-to-door, pounding to alert residents to take to high ground. Some moved into Wapello High School. On the day the dike split in six places below Wapello, a volunteer — patroling the dike in his all-terrain rig —hit the brakes. A crevasse had split the dike, tumbling him into deep trouble. He escaped the muddy swirl, but the monstrous gush of water swept his vehicle to the top of a tree. For some small towns, all the back-wrenching work, the sandbagging, foretold a doomed effort that will sting the memory for years.

"One week, I worked 98 hours sandbagging. What a waste," said Mike Abbot of Keithsburg.

Even the U.S. Army Corps of Engineers in Rock Island admitted that — in many communities — the man-made berms and sandbagging would have only prolonged the inevitable along rivers like the Mississippi, the Illinois, the Rock and Des Moines.

The Associated Press reported on the day of the Quad-City crest that time, high water, poor maintenance — something — eventually will undo the best of humankind's work.

"We're learning that," Gary Loss, assistant chief of the Army Corps of Engineers, Rock Island District, told AP.

It was a grim reminder for the future.

At least 200 homes were damaged in Buffalo, where angry homeowners kept sightseers away by firing bb shots at cars.

Right: Volunteers struggle to plug a gaping hole in a leaky dike in Andalusia, Ill.

Above: With a flag to mark the Fourth of July, Kathy Webster grabs for a fallen sandbag as the windblown floodwaters slowly tear apart her dike. Moments later, it gave way, pouring into two Davenport businesses, Auto Parts Co. and Solar Vision.

Right: Pumps strain to keep ahead of the rising river at the Front Street Brewery in Davenport. They lost the battle, and employees were forced to dump the vats of beer brewing in the basement.

The great beer swim

A lifetime dream for Craig "Smitty" Smith: He went swimming in beer, lapping up the brew with each lap. Front Street Brewery, in Davenport, one of the immersed businesses along River Drive, had to empty all of its home made beer down the drains. Glub-glub-glub went the big copper vats, but the drain couldn't handle 1,000 gallons of beer all at once. The beer reached a swimmable four feet in the basement and Smitty, a cook at the place, leaped in and went swimming.

A worried president comes calling

He was concerned, deeply concerned. His manner and his worries showed. A president of the United States doesn't spend four hours and 15 minutes in a drizzling city on the 4th of July without having a mission in mind.

The renegade flood of 1993 had reached its first crest of the summer on that holiday, an inauspicious way to greet a president.

Bill Clinton studied all the water dousing Davenport. "It is amazing, and it is a very tough problem. I've seen a lot of it in my life, and this is about as bad as it gets."

At first, he stared down at "Lake Davenport" from the Centennial Bridge. It was a sea of greenish, cocoa-colored water.

"I'm sorry about all of the water. I know what you are going through, and I'm very sorry," the president said.

He stood on the bridge, arms folded in an Arkansas tuck, like one of the good old boys. He wore cowboy boots and blue jeans, and to offer any needed support, Agriculture Secretary Mike Espy was at his side. Espy, too, was in blue jeans. Davenport Mayor Pat Gibbs joined them, and he later said that he felt mightily overdressed because he was in a blue blazer, necktie and chinos.

In some manners of thinking, it was an incongruous visit. The last time a U.S. President stopped in the Quad-Cities was five years earlier. President Reagan came to talk about drought. Now, here was a U.S. President talking about too much water.

Always the smiling hand-shaker, President Clinton worked the crowds, pumping palms all the way to West Third and Gaines streets.

"God bless you, Mr. President," called Dee Canfield of Moline. Angela Cretty, 10, of Davenport — in her sunback dress — hurried to get his autograph. He told her "Just a minute, honey." When he signed her paper, he said that she was cute. She held the autograph closely and said, "He's a great president. I think he cares about us."

Caring. That was the general mood. People who were tired of fighting a flood that wouldn't say no were glad to see a president who cared enough to share their worries — and on a holiday!

A long motorcade (22 cars) wound its way from

Left: President Clinton gives the "OK" sign as he and Mike Espy, secretary of agriculture, meet with Iowa farmers during one of the president's trips to the flood-ravaged Midwest.

Left: After viewing the flood damage, President Clinton met with farmers at the home of Don and Elaine Schneckloth near Eldridge, Iowa. He promised $1.2 billion of aid, an amount he doubled within days.

Left: Nine-year-old Joe
Schneckloth shares a
secret and a bale of hay
with the President of the
United States.

Next pages: On a
drizzly July 4, 1993,
President Clinton
surveys downtown
Davenport from
Centennial Bridge.
River Drive is in the
background. "I've seen
a lot of it in my life," he
said, "and this is about
as bad as it gets." With
him are, from left, U.S.
Army Corps of
Engineers Col. Albert
Krause, Davenport
Mayor Pat Gibbs, Iowa
Gov. Terry Branstad
(blue shirt), and U.S.
Agriculture Secretary
Mike Espy. (White
House pool photo)

Davenport into the gray-green countryside for the central purpose of the visit. A thin mist was falling. Along the way, the president took a good look at swamped fields and low pastures that had turned into lakes big enough to stock with crappies. The destination was the farm of Don and Elaine Schneckloth, retired farmers from near Eldridge, Iowa.

This was down-home Io-way. A canopy-like tent with straw on the ground to soak up the mud was headquarters between the barn and the house. About a hundred farmers and neighbors gathered to tell their problems to a listening president and his secretary of agriculture.

"I felt he was well-informed about everything," said Dean Bousselot, a farmer from Dixon, Iowa, a small town up the road a piece. "He seemed to be sincere about helping the farmers. There's only so much he can do, but it sounds like he is trying."

The president promised aid, quickly escalating into many billions.

For the dozens of the nation's media present, the scene looked like a set for "Hee Haw." The president sat on a bale of hay, and for a spell was joined by 9-year-old Joe Schneckloth, a grandson of Don and Elaine. Joe was getting antsy. He sucked on a stem of straw, fidgeted, yawned and once caught himself holding his hands to his ears. It was a good laugh for all the good country folks who had gathered around.

The Schneckloths were awed and amazed to host the president.

"Usually, on the 4th of July, we have a family picnic," said Elaine, who insisted upon wearing a dress that was red, white and blue.

It was no quickie in-and-out, but a good old chew-the-rag exchange for farmers to get a lot of things off their chest. Glen Keppy, a Davenport farmer, stood to thank the president for caring enough about their situation to come to Iowa.

President Clinton's visit was the mountain top, but the plight of flooded Midwest farmers brought a plethora of politicians to the Quad-Cities — Jim Edgar, the governor of Illinois, and Terry Branstad, the governor of Iowa — and ag aides and commerce secretaries.

Iowa Gov. Branstad was to later sum it up quite well:

"I know of no area that is totally spared. I think it is clearly the worst natural disaster in the history of the state."

Bill Clinton

Flooded fields

Everywhere in the countryside, enormous masses of water.

The lure of the land has always been a hand on the plow and the firm feeling of good, black dirt beneath the feet. In the summer of 1993, the feeling turned to mud.

In the beginning, we slogged through a moist March and the land became saturated.

By mid-July, when the flood crests had passed, our rainfall had already measured more than a foot above normal. By early July, the old blue-bibbed farmer would say, corn should be knee-high. That old adage had worn itself out. Usually, by mid-July, shoulder high was talked about at the grain elevator and feed store.

But by mid-summer of 1993, tens and tens of thousands of acres had yet to be planted.

In the beginning, the farmland itself was a worried torment. Then, farmers around Muscatine and Morrison switched their thrust to equipment. They rolled combines and tractors out of machine sheds, to the safety of farm bluffs. On the Illinois side of the Quad-Cities, water swept through 30,000 acres of prime farmland in a day. Farmers could be seen tearing up their corn crops to build dikes around their homes and farm buildings.

Listen to Darwin Krebs, who farms near Stockton, Iowa: "I planted one field twice this year, then gave up." He lost hundreds of acres to flooding. Rich, black, Iowa loam turned to gumbo swamp. Neighbors tried to make him laugh by calling his farm "Lake Darwin."

Soaked figures can be dull, but they add up enormously to sudden losses. One break in the levee, near Oquawka, Ill., flooded 3,000 acres in an hour. In Jackson County, Iowa, the raging Maquoketa River swamped 4,000 acres in one swoop. The Maquoketa River hit its highest point in a half-century, with water dousing the lowlands after a six-inch rain upstream at Delhi.

William Faulkner once wrote: "... At floodtime, the river was now doing what it liked to do, had waited patiently for years in order to do, as a mule will work for you 10 years for the privilege of kicking you once."

Some crops, on high land, did well. Others, saturated by rain and soaked by the muddy rise and fall of creeks, yellowed and died. On that landmark

Left: A farm north of Muscatine becomes an island in the swollen Iowa River.

*Above: Bob Carter and
his son, Tim, gaze at
their 400 acres of
flooded farmland near
Princeton, Iowa.*

Following pages: The Iowa River surges at Wapello. In Louisa County, flood waters chased 2,000 people from their homes.

Above: Barges wait at an isolated grain elevator at Oquawka, Ill.

Left: A flooded corn field stands as testimony of the devastation caused to thousands of square miles of rich Midwest farmland.

4th of July — when the corn was to be knee high and the skyrockets shooting into the sky—Whiteside County in Illinois had 22,000 acres underwater. On that day, Scott County had between 15,000 and 20,000 acres submerged in one form or another.

"It's always been a continual hassle to farm," said Tim Lundy of rural Savanna, Ill. "This year has been the worst. We had to give up to 600 acres that did not get planted. We've exhausted all options."

Jim Endress, a farm management staffer at the University of Illinois, said farmers are frightened and disgusted and worried about going to the bank. "They've gone through bad times, but nothing quite like this."

As the water receded, flooded farmers did some unprecedented acts. You could hear the boom of dynamite as farmers blasted dikes — once intended to keep the water from the fields — now being blown open to let the water out.

Hellish, and not business as usual

The strange craft kept drifting up and down and around on silent Davenport's River Drive where semis and cars usually buzz an incessant roar. The boaters had it all to themselves. What a bizarre bunch of gondoliers guided this ferryboat, a pontoon of sorts, built by employees of ABC Supply Co. The job was to move the company's building supplies to high ground. The employees had no oars. They struggled with 2 x 6 boards to paddle the home-made craft, moving $500,000 of materials as floodwaters inched into the warehouse.

Elsewhere, the food scene surged into a far less amiable spectacle. Auto Parts Co. and Solar Vision, two neighboring River Drive businesses, yelled for help against the forces. They lost, and in a vain but valiant cry, made a big sign for the roof in hopes that President Clinton might catch a glance when he flew over Davenport. The sign said: "S.O.S. Mr. President."

Not everyone lost the war so tragically.

Up and down River Drive, and along Second Street, and finally Third Street in Davenport, businesses fought the flood. Most of the time, they were victorious in one soaking way or another — like ABC Supply and its clumsy but effective Venetian rafts. ABC had found a "dry" temporary warehouse, and employees tediously but cheerily poled materials through the water on 12-foot-long floating docks.

"We went into the ship-building business to keep the company in business," said Larry Wakeland, sweating in rubber waders.

Davenport financial institutions pumped water from their basements. Downriver, Buffalo Savings Bank moved the money and efficiently set up a teller line in the art room of Buffalo Elementary School. Davenport Peterson Paper Co., a focus point for dozens of national TV cameras, boated paper out of the five-storied flood-locked plant, and then to trucks waiting on high-and-dry streets. They didn't miss an order.

Clinton, with its floodwall, kept its powder dry. Muscatine, with its floodwall and floodgates, got a sloshing but did not float away. The floor buckled

Left: Thousands of
water pumps were put
to work up and down
the Mississippi in a
desperate, but often
futile battle. Victor
Cardoso of Iowa-
Illinois Gas and
Electric Co. checks one
of the machines on
Davenport's Main
Street.

*Above: Still open
despite the floodwaters
that climb toward his
front door, Jim Foster
of Mr. Jim's 1-Hour
Dry Cleaners in
Muscatine, watches the
scene with dismay.
Muscatine Journal
photo by Tom Korte.*

in the basement of Muscatine Carriage House Decorating Center, and bubbled through the sandstone basement wall of Wilson's Shoe Store, crawling up the wet steps. Always, the basements go first. Charlie's Deli in Muscatine gurgled into a "swimming pool" with six feet of water in the basement.

Bottled Mississippi River Flood Water, Vintage 1993, became a big seller to benefit Muscatine's American Red Cross chapter.

Hawkeye Lumber Co. in Muscatine was hard hit. From the air, the yard of jumbled floating lumber looked like toothpicks bobbing in a stock tank of muddy water.

In downtown Muscatine, what an unlikely scene when motorists, unable to find parking for cars, boated to work and tethered aluminum crafts to parking meter posts.

The staggering battle to save neighbor-businesses

Sign language

Floodwater trickled at the edges of the new Mark of the Quad-Cities in Moline. Sandbaggers filled 'em up in exchange for free tickets to Bon Jovi. Some wag put up a sign calling the place, "The High Water Mark."

Lots of signs, too, on flooded Quad-City area streets: "Free Car Wash." Clinton's Riverboat Days went on as usual with a slogan, "Come Hell or High Water."

At TC's East in the Village of East Davenport, a banner encouraged the hangers-on: "All Drinks, All Burgers 65 Cents in Memory of the Flood of '65." Peggy Sue's, the ala "Beach Boys" bistro that muddled through to stay open in all that water, had a sign that said: "Guaranteed Riverside Seating — Water Views at All Times."

Down on the Davenport levee, photographers clicked at the parking lot sign for the exited-President, gambling boat. The sign said: "Lot Full." It sure was — full of water.

*Above: Using a jet ski
to patrol downtown
Davenport, Scott
County sheriff's deputy
Bobbie Aye exchanges
information with Shelly
Nichols, owner of
Chet's Tavern.*

Above: The welcome mat is always out in downtown Davenport—even when it's a little soggy.

Left: Shaun LeMaster joins 75 other youths from Arrowhead Ranch in a vain attempt to protect John O'Donnell Stadium in Davenport.

Solar Vision and Auto Parts Co. became a knock-down, drag-out epic on Davenport River Drive. Steve Webster (Solar) and Howard Tatge (Auto Parts) strained for sleepless, 48-hour stretches to build impregnable sandbag walls. Neither company had "his" or "her" sandbags. The two shared survival. They mounted a flag that waved "Fort Apache" in big letters and the national media cheered with front page photos.

The battle of Solar Vision and Auto Parts emerged as a saga of how all of America shifted into gear to help Davenport survive the flood of 1993. "While we struggled," Steve said, "I got a call from a customer in Missouri who had seen us on national news. The parking lot flowed in two feet of water, and the flood lapped at our doors. The caller, understanding our urgency, said, 'I've got two pumps.' He arrived, eight hours later from Missouri with the pumps. We had renewed hope."

The hope did not last. Flood walls burst. National Guardsmen yelled, "Get the hell out of here."

Steve said, emotionally: "We tried to beat it. Maybe next time."

Previous pages: Kris and Larry Zellmer manage a smile amid the misery along 179th Street Place in Pleasant Valley, Iowa.

Above: The irony of a "Dead End" sign, and a sign that cautioned against sitting or stopping, was evident as rising floodwaters engulfed a bridge in Hampton, Ill.

Right: Oquawka, Ill., where the city council adjourned to repair the levee.

'Fats' and the sandbags

They called him "Fats" Collins. His nickname told his portly size. He casually hefted 40-pound sandbags in Keithsburg, Ill., pleased to do it. Fats turned into one of those unlikely heroes of the Great Flood of 1993. Hundreds of prisoners were "unlocked" to work the flood. The small towns said "much obliged." Many residents became friends with the inmates. They brought them cookies and fudge and promised to write.

Fats is serving 6 1/2 years for voluntary manslaughter. He and about 100 others from East Moline Correctional Center and Hill Correctional Center at Galesburg, Ill., worked weeks beside the volunteers in Keithsburg. They received time for good behavior and citizenship.

Downstream at Wever, Iowa, 100 prisoners from Iowa State Penitentiary at Ft. Madison filled sandbags to bolster a levee. They worked all day for two weeks. At 3 p.m. daily, a flatbed truck carried the inmates to a gray prison bus. A corrections officer called off each inmate's name, and each man got a can of pop before stepping onto the prison bus.

Heroes and big hearts

Will Rogers said it: "We can't all be heroes because somebody has to sit on the curb and clap as they go by." The Quad-Cities put on its water wings and life jackets to become hero country during the "Great Flood of 1993." People never tire of greatness, in big or small doses. The "Great Flood of 1993" proved that the Quad-Cities—while at its grim worst — could show that its people rated the best. And the common person, without stars or medals, as always emerged as the hero.

Barbara Cirillo will not forget that early morning in July when she had only 80 cents in her pocket; when the gas gauge in her 1976 Nova showed empty, and she had a crawling feeling of panic. National Guardsmen had told her to leave her home in the Garden Addition of Davenport. In the damp darkness, she and her brother, a boyfriend, a dog and cat climbed into her Chevy. Davenport Police Chief Steve Lynn reached into his pocket and handed her $5 for gasoline. In that time of need, the Quad-Cities had no shortage of heroes.

Everyone wanted to help, and it was like Joan Baez used to sing, "Oh, action is the antidote to despair, the only antidote to despair." People didn't talk. They acted. Eighteen Red Cross trucks rolled into the region, and volunteer nurses never left the Red Cross shelter in the Army Reserve Center on Division Street in Davenport. Cafeteria workers in the Davenport Community School District gave up summer vacation days to make 1,000 meals a day for flood workers — burgers and chicken nuggets and cupcakes. Everywhere, the sandbaggers sweated and shoveled hoisted the silky-slick sacks to become unlikely heroes. Manet Seguin showed up to help build the embankment at the Village of East Davenport. A tiny woman, she shooed away the husky Guardsmen. "I'm plenty strong," she insisted. She worked for two hours. She is 91.

More than 300 National Guardsmen — in their summer camo fatigues — worked sometimes he-

Left: National Guardsmen in makeshift barracks at Iowa-American Water Co., Davenport. They sandbagged in shifts to keep the river out of the water supply.

81

A singing stranger

The pastor of First Baptist Church in Rock Island announced that the day's special music would be canceled because the singer had fallen ill. He smiled: "I don't suppose we have anyone in the church ready to come up here on a moment's notice and sing."

A stranger's hand raised. Up walked a clean-cut young man, with close-cropped hair. He sang a cappella. The congregation applauded. They back-patted him as a professional.

"Who are you?" they asked.

"I attend church in any city where I'm assigned," he answered. "I'm a Marine, in charge of communications for President Clinton's visit to the Quad-Cities."

The work drags through the night as the National Guard and volunteers build a sandbag wall in the Village of East Davenport.

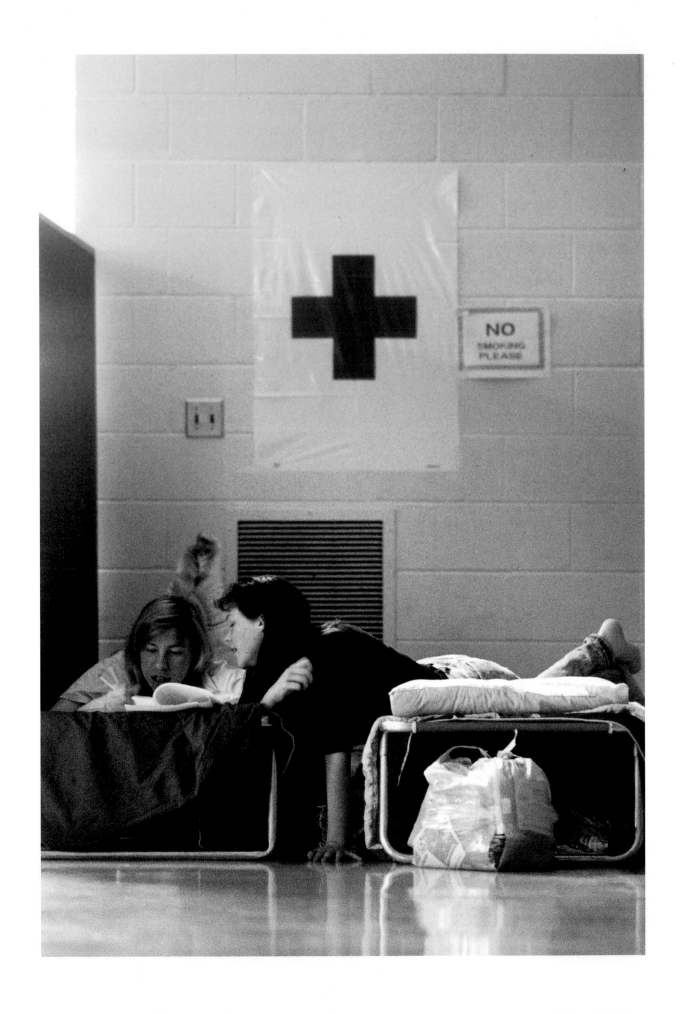

Above: A weary Sandra Payne and her daughter, Kathryn, listen to instructions at a disaster aid application office in Davenport.

Left: Scharie Hoffman, 17, left, and Kim Burns, 14, share a quiet moment in the Red Cross evacuation shelter Army Reserve Center in Davenport.

roic, sometimes hum-drum shifts without a mumble or a grumble.

"I have a great view of the river," cracked Sgt. Michael Bisdorf, "but sleeping here on cots can be a little strange." He and 50 other Guardsmen, on duty or on call 24 hours a day, protected the antiseptic-clean Iowa-American Water Co. plant in Davenport. While a million-plus dollars of local flood assistance came in — perhaps from those out of harm's way — the little heroes kept emerging. Old Country Buffet in Davenport handed out a thousand passes for dinners to flood victims. Harris Pizza fed hungry flood fighters with all the cheese and pepperoni they wanted. Ryan's Family Steak House kept the Red Cross shelter well supplied with sugar and oatmeal cookies. The AMOCO station at Kimberly Road and Brady Street gave $10 worth of free gas to those hit by the flood. Phillips Petroleum sent letters to its Quad-City customers, offering deferred credit card payments to flood victims. Anheuser-Busch donated 4,000 cases of canned fresh drinking water. Parishioners rallied up to their necks in water to save the home of Rev. James Conroy in Buffalo,

When life becomes too much

Times arrive when endurance reaches the snapping point. The Elwess family survived triple tragedies. Mike, 26, and Karen, 22, lived with his parents in Davenport's Garden Addition in 1990. A flash flood hit, and Mike carried their baby girl out of water higher than his waist.

Karen and Mike moved to Florida, to have their home hit by Hurricane Andrew last year. The cost of living was too much for them, so they returned to Davenport — back to the Garden Addition — and faced by misfortune once again. Garden Addition was evacuated in the summer flood of 1993. The family ended up at the Red Cross Shelter on Division Street; their two dogs and two cats curled up at the Mississippi Valley Fairgrounds pet shelter.

Above: Davenport police officer Lyle Wiggins tells Randy and Angie Cook and Regina Butler that they must leave their Garden Addition homes. The danger of a flood-weakened dike forced the order to evacuate more than 600 residents.

Right: Flood victims wait their turn at Red Cross headquarters in Rock Island High School.

Iowa. With 40 tons of sand, they piled sandbags five feet high as a wall against the Mississippi River. In thanks, Rev. Conroy held a sodden picnic for those who saved his house. When the floodwaters left, he offered to give the rescuers the sandbags as gifts of thanks.

*Above: On Front Street
in Buffalo, Iowa,
residents watch
anxiously as storm
clouds gather — again.*

Above: Water spreads in all directions above Muscatine, Iowa.

Left: Railroad tracks vanish in downtown Burlington, Iowa.

Following pages. Larry Miller, an employee of the Davenport Park and Recreation Department, scrapes away a thick layer of sludge and slime left behind when flood waters receded from the outfield of John O'Donnell Stadium.

Stop that train with a .22 rifle

Lay that pistol down, boys, lay that pistol down.

Any number of incidents riled the edgy folks in water-logged Buffalo, Iowa, just downstream from Davenport. People splattered BB guns at cars going around barricades.

They really got their dander up when the Soo Line Railroad tried to take a train through town on the watery tracks near Front Street, carrying 30 carloads of phosphoric acid.

Residents feared the track unsafe after being underwater for at least a week. When Front Street residents heard the train's whistle, they hollered for it to stop.

Some waded onto the tracks, waving protest. One man even went out on the rails with a .22-caliber rifle, said Cheryl Meador of Buffalo.

"My husband was out with his .22 but he did not shoot. He just pointed in the air," she said.

The folks won. The train stopped and went back to the station. The railroad said the reason was because there was too much water on the tracks.

Above: Silent figures in John Bloom's bronze sculpture watch the rising Mississippi from behind a sandbag wall in Davenport.

Left: The Mississippi stretches miles past the banks of Ninemile Island near Dubuque, Iowa.

Acknowledgements...

A flood is an ugly thing to cover. You don't stand on the riverbank and get stories. You pull on waders, or climb in a boat, and live with and work with and sympathize with the people who are trying to survive.

On some days, the Quad-City Times had more than a dozen reporters covering the flood, up and down the Mississippi River and its tributaries.

As it rained and rained, they became accustomed to being wet. The reporters were cold at night, walking the levees.

At anxious moments, they helped fill sandbags. They lived a part of this drama.

Here are the reporters who covered and front-line editors who handled the "Great Flood of 1993" for the Quad-City Times:

Barb Arland-Fye, Linda Barr, Ross Bielema, Deborah Brasier, Craig Brown, Cheri Bustos, Chris Cashion, Lisa Cloat, Linda Cook, Monte Cox, Carie Dann, Jennifer DeWitt, Bj Elsner, Mark Feeney, Alma Gaul, Shenetha Hannah, Helen Hanson, Bill Jacobs, Clark Kauffman, Sara Miller, Lee Nelson, Mary Nevans-Pederson, Kathie Obradovich, Rick Rector, Scott Reeder, Mark Ridolfi, Jim Rudisill, Doug Schorpp, Holly A. Smith, Susie Snyder, Ed Tibbetts, Beth Vanderkerckhove, Linda Watson, John Willard.

(The material for this book was assembled from their stories and written by Bill Wundram.)

95

Above: The photographers of the Quad-City Times who contributed to this book, and who covered the flood from its very start, are, from left, Jeff Cook, Greg Boll, John Schultz, Leslie Hahn, Shane Keyser, Larry Fisher and Craig Chandler.

Right: Bill Wundram, columnist for the Quad-City Times, has written about life along the Mississippi, at high tide and low, since 1944. He assembled the material for this book from the news coverage by the staff of the Quad-City Times.

Below: Aerial photography by Larry Mayer, Billings Montana Gazette.